STUDY IN TRANSHUMANCE

Roaring Fork Passage
Grace; The snakes and the dogs
House of Eagles
Yana
Somata
The Composition of Glass
The Excesses The Caprices
Courtesan of Seizure
Chromatic Defacement
Venaculture
The Ideation
Imperfect Poverty
The Valley of Cranes
The World's Description

STUDY IN TRANSHUMANCE

PHILLIP FOSS

Singing Horse Press 2019

ISBN 978-0-935162-87-5

The cover photo is by the author.

"kingfisher as dragonfly" first appeared in *Hambone* and "the odor of snow" in *The Volta.*

Thanks and apologies to the authors whose language I appropriated in the sequence *Vinteuil's sonata:* Hans Jonas, Alexander Scriabin, Igor Stravinsky, Hazart Inayat Kahn, and Marcel Proust.

Singing Horse Press
12170 Ragweed Street
San Diego, CA 92129

Singing Horse Press books are available from the publisher at singinghorsepress.com or from Small Press Distribution (800) 869-7553 or at www.spdbooks.org.

CONTENTS

STUDY IN TRANSHUMANCE

(the practice of observing mountains run)

SELF PORTRAIT AS MOTH

you woke with your face heavy
with frost but it was only moonlight redolent

of artemisia an inebriate she said you
have no history the faces eroded landscape

deflated stars no longer ideas
merely the black wall singing

in a language you have misplaced women
within the shades of bluegreengrey

because you missed the moonlight
it was seated at the table next to you

dressed as a woman
she said sea was infinite in seeing

and regret where all actors depart
across a denuded shore to return

to a memory they glimpse approaching as gesture
of dust on the horizon which they must reach

solely by sense of touch she said why morning
star rises in your irises

~ ~ ~

THE WORLD AS DESIRE AND AMNESIA

because the oak forest was merely actualized light was an easy metamorphosis
to accept but unaccountable for her beauty I said

but such is the problem of reflection I deceived myself in seeing the moth
fluttering down as light from night stars

because the light reflecting from her face was that of a blue callus lily
this being the provenance of hylozoic faith

so the template of my perfect ideation is slipping this is merely erosion
corrosion of years' failure to think clearly leaf's vein

because past is merely imagining an apricot tree in bloom
during some year I've forgotten

who is speaking here where earth is covered with white blossoms surely no
one I apprehend but if I move my head laterally the world changes color

air is brown with dust small birds plummet downwind bees retreat
to mexico thus my mind is merely a species of dirt

perhaps a wind driven cloud sped through a granite fissure and said god or said no
thing the initial fallacy is in the prescription of vibration's causality

I don't even know if galaxies or stars or pebbles vibrate perhaps
in such ignorance can belief resonate

for example using simple geometry I determined there is no edifice calibrated
as past or no welcoming artifice designated as potential

that left me with the problem of rapid white cumulus rushing
my head so I pick up my body and pretend or it is all magic

as when I vibrate air in an empty bottle and point it toward a half set sun
and am awed that it always fills with fireflies

or there were moon shadows beneath every tree every blade of grass beneath
my body even its enunciations similar to feeling the conversations of mycelium

because I fell down into memory the banal or sublime falling leaf or bird or planet
is unseen and even crickets red arts even moths conspire

because I watch the wooden table revert to tree on its leafed branch is a meadow
lark which sings a melody I cannot contain in my palm

because in eating the wild mushroom its mountain enters my blood
because her transparent skin merely mimics the fluency of her skull

~ ~~

SYMMETRIES OF RECOIL

you walked out onto the river seeking white
geese and realized the waves were solid silver

with the backs of spawning fish
this was why the sky collapsed when you shouted

begin the end
then how many thousands of times did you acknowledge

the eastern sunrise always naming the west
north thus its mutilated rising in the south and this tipped

the planet in your spine so you sat
down to white bread and white butter

but morning's lilac breeze tilted
your vision toward a denmark

with ocean and perfumed skirts
where perhaps it was the arctic winters huddled

in the aura of coal when you tried to memorize the eddas
in tongues that made you fall down

made you mad you will forget everything there
is a darkness that has been sidling up beside you

since you accosted word from air
inarticulate more a presence

like pressure from a forge or glance
yet you wandered the countryside bombed to ruins delighted

at bits of song bits of bone you found scattered
colder than hailstones but in this painting

aerial birds are replaced
by ouzels feeding underwater in melted

snow they have not been granted individual names
by any god as you have not in retribution

each resurrected horse you gave a new name
when beneath you they fell again arose fell again arose

and you rode unscathed toward the full
moon impaled on a stunted pine where your room

was walled with weapons this was the sacred
garden its geometries extended into cosmos thereby reconciling

absurd theories performed in future lives
where you realized there was nothing in life for you

to do rain caused the grass to grow grass
caused the cattle to grow cattle caused you to grow

then they all fell down they all fell down stream I wasn't there
it is all hearsay that you casually picked

up a bright rock mere bit of fallen star
and the milky way absently absorbed your face

THE ODOR OF SNOW

the river-cobble wall is a method of ascribing
value to the trajectory of moonlight beyond the glass

only iterations of force or a whirlwind of energy named
names to draw limits to its confusion yellow-

winged blackbird lavender bee-plant rufus
hummingbird: these are sounds you are

the articulate carapace stuttering in the coals while
arctic wind gessos the mountains

on hands and knees you stare at rain drops reflecting
moon because cicadas are singing the sound of tectonic plates

sliding windless dawn stem of yellow-flowered groundsel vibrates audibly
harmonic or sentience corvis comments that the brown sparrows

perched on the rope are dried leaves of a climbing vine the premise
of ornithology is the say xylophone apparently incongruous

other than decibels to call the music of stars or plumage
displayed say red pinions say blue tail then color or you

were describing the sound of struck metal or the way a bird can say

there is a vertical line where memory
and sentience separate this is a musical

note exaggerated attended by a mind unworded
in thought the way the skin of a woman

is the emission of light when musical sound
leaves symbolic representation sound is two

meanings neither merely a mockingbird
a sitar ratchets off worlds that do not mean

harmonies or the two dimples above the buttocks
are articulate on the notion of ecstatic music

there is a cricket singing beneath the metal pot it is
the memory of bronze

so no willow self mind is aspen then white
is where you found anemones pulsating in tide pools

this dispenses knowing of knowledge the way
blood accelerates through the body at the thought

of being dead feathers flutter from flocks of migrating
south birds you name you

observer of your perceptions like the concept of you can see
your hand covering winter sun in its early setting

dissolution drives fecundity of the world to know
to unknown: you stop on a mental image say a leaf orange

with green veins and you prevent it falling to litter
and dissolution of unity or your cognition

finds cello seeping into your chest this is hearing
as when you open your mouth to speak the sands

of sediment taste like lime: this can be described as the way
light articulates its idea of image through eye as a way of laughing

white bark becomes pictograph declaring emotion while
white geese are declarations of sky roses and the white snow

is a disguise where nothing is seen in this seeing through any gap
in memory where sky is always blue and the sky is nevertheless blue

and there is always a gap between cliffs where one sees
the future as merely banal artifacts of living strewn

along the shore of a blue lake in some country that never
existed as either bone awl stone pestle or necklace bead of blue

stone to force
blind wrong mind

nothing matters the deceit folly caress
of sublime all merely a dropped pot its mica

reflecting in a pine woods for a thousand
years brushed by birds' voices or breath

of inland sea

hands smell of spruce sap

and you perceive a violent blizzard approaching
down the river basin unclothed by name or word

this version occurs beneath an eclipsed moon

crazed wall slipped with clay is not a wall
but a green tea cup set vertically you can hear yourself

if you talk into it stories of mountains of mist
and granite and beautiful wraiths who beckon you in languages

barbarian and bodhidharma's wall was the same concave
mirror to reflect his seeing nothing or merely thought: if he moved

with his right his left responded; if he thought
with his left his right galloped so much to accumulate

to hoard: acres of air miles
of light sheets of falling laughter

earthen house on billion year old continent floats
west toward the pacific sans

sail sans compass no pilot I but victim of magnetics solar
flares oscillating poles where clouds are a series of striations muscle

moving contra my sailing meaning earth and sky drift contra
meaning water comes from the west dying sails toward the sea

this happened before continuing to happen I remember the prairie
described as a sea floating west you remember the grasses

gestured toward the east yet if you move too far west it is east or the soul
shuttles on magma west into night

VINTEUIL'S SONATA

what the sound immediately discloses
is not an object but a dynamical event at the locus
of the object and thereby mediately the state
the object is in at the moment

of that occurrence whir of a cicada invisible within purple
aster man and dogs believe snake even though
the sun's raining particles are barely audible

the object-reference of sounds is not provided by the sounds
as such and it transcends the performance of mere hearing or the man

found her body submerged
in a pool of air singing
of the immortality of extinguished stars striking
the lake's black ice like a redundant
glass bell because he is solely that sound

all indications of existents of enduring
things beyond the sound-events themselves
 are extraneous to their own nature

thus he does not differentiate that the sound
of leaves falling beneath almond trees
is the sound of falling birds

I *want to augment sounds* the body
is a nonmetallic tuning fork *with the parallelism*
of light every living or dead thing leaves
a residual vibration *but no* everything
is a sympathetic resonator *I want counterpoint*
because any sound is a form of speech *the lights pursue*
their melody the blue jay doesn't sing it speaks *and the music*
goes on with its because blue is the color *now*
I want a contrapuntalism of all the different lines
of art of arterial blood

the phenomenon of music is nothing
other than a phenomenon of speculation

there is nothing
in this expression that should frighten you

the elements at which this speculation aims
are those of sound and time music is inconceivable

apart from those two elements
because there are *two kinds of music: one which evolves*

parallel to the process of ontological time embracing
and penetrating it inducing in the mind

a feeling of euphoria the other runs ahead of or counter
to this process it is not self contained

in each momentary tonal unit it dislocates
the centers of attraction and gravity and sets itself up in the unstable

and this fact makes it particularly adaptable
since *all music being nothing but a succession of impulses*

and repose drawing together separation of poles
of attraction in a way determine the respiration of music

will I then have to lose myself in this abyss of freedom
to what shall I cling in order to escape

the dizziness that seizes me before the virtuality
of this infinitude

experienced only the physical quality of the sounds
secreted by the instruments

music the word we use in our everyday language
is nothing less than the picture of the beloved all actions
and movements made in the visible and invisible
world are musical they are made up of vibrations
pertaining to a certain plane of existence what makes us
feel drawn to music is that our whole being
is music: our mind our body the nature in which we live
the nature that has made us all that is beneath
and around us is all music

below the little line of the violin slender unyielding
compact and commanding he had seen the mass
of the piano part all at once struggling to rise in a liquid
swell multiform undivided smooth and colliding
like the purple tumult of the waves when the moonlight
charms them and lowers their pitch by half a tone

sound and color are one they are two aspects of life
life and light are one where sound is colour
it is most visible and least audible and where color
is sound it is most audible and least visible

~ ~ ~

BIOLUMINESCENCE

the white bark enters my eyes that statement is the same
as white lilac blossoms have closed the door to this house the voices

in the forest are those of trees accompanying their ceaseless birth they
are dependent on lightning as phenomenology as rain or a woman

walking through that forest hears her description roll before her
as mycelium as breeze as gossip (you allow one finger to enter

the gills of the mushroom) that the mushrooms flowers trees clouds
are watching her walking through toward away is obvious yet she

craves more separateness not clothes loaded with spore seed rain
merely carrying all others' sex to virgin ground this luminescence

is olfactory is liminal auditory tactile yes prescient I once observed a woman
whose lips glowed white while walking talking in darkness:

"into the thunderstorm spadefoot toads sang"

silver haired prostitute sings rhymes red sunset
ricochets between windows selling food great blue heron

strides through shallows looks up at constellations seeing
moon as a goddess who orchestrates the world's waves you found

a coin wedged in the stone upon which she sat bouncing
bloodied moonlit and the rhymes are sounds they perceive as colors

or a rain so fine its impact on steel is soundless she sang
the only measurement of life will be taken with light never time

six juncos jump up and down in a head-
sized remnant of smoke-glazed snow

you are breathing atmospheric ocean

never silence always the professing of birds ontology
of heretics through a wind you will later describe

as bellicose though her eyes' smile
displayed not even the least luminescence this is where

you will abandon the suffrage of duration shore
up the tattered colors of your soul and sail for cold lava

wind ascended leaf or russet finch:
movement necessitates sentience

beyond the blue mountain bluer a suppurating
the black mountain: thus the supplicant calls
it pilgrim or lost in shedding of water

you are it or he ameliorating transpiration
of every breathing mind call it you sentient
seasonality spring perhaps a kind of woman

sound exclusively province of breeze you see
your inverted body reflected in drops
of water falling from the beak of kingfisher

I herd my animal upslope into the blue
and a progressive retardation of civil of language
like the child grasping the cherry sapling

jumping updown vulture overhead
conversing his eyes follow my eyes
in walking fire is defeated

I saw viscous light burst from the body it must
be a memory of forgetting the way you see
a fir cone floating downstream aided by cicada singing

now there are no antecedents only
memory and genetics pertain hagiographies
brittle pages rise into the light as a
swarm of dust motes

the speaking dead form a kind of helmet
which you wear; not bronze with horsehair
tassel but liquid perhaps red or
black depending on the moon

the black orange winged tarantula hawk
informed me my land has been owned
for a million years by ants

the golden light shining into my eyes
from the bush is the throat of a
hummingbird its frenzied declaration

~ ~ ~

ARTICULATED HELMET

this steel and cedar gate is a metaphorical opening ingress
egress toward away from a world uncontrolled human
construct of language crippling cognition it is not a blue
gate but green which some languages refuse to delineate even
as it is said to yaw

or the raku wall is crazed
this is the conclusion to the argument

because shadows solidify
into inarticulate vibrating objects

thus water and glass are synonyms

predawn yellow light seeping up from ground
beneath bald trees whoosh of stroking birds navigating
stars is a dialogue where words like heart have no
meaning where both mouth and hand are empty

thus her objective was to cease thinking
in words or she thought in artificial compartments

when physically bird=wind=insect=
water=seed=bifurcating into an endless ricochet

do not name it
and it exists in its singular purity

thus no "no"

in peripheral vision hummingbird choreography
is what body knows dynamic of air to earth
merely sliding scale of color avocet as orange

or asteroid tumbling toward earth expresses
the same meaning as vulture perched on fence
post spreading its wings to first ray of dawn

thus you leap over the shadow of a flying
raven not to interrupt its flight or
your back is blackened

the way sunset lured
mushrooms up the mountains

since this is the past it is faded
yet you remember sole crow on a field of snow
but only its unrelenting monologue

all speech means
nothing it is merely the rattling
of symbols inside a yellow gourd

one crow on a field has forgotten
dualism forgotten symmetry
has no believe

I dwell in my absence who
is speaking tarantula skunk bumblebee

the voice of the cricket is not the voice
of the lark they are different both are yellow
languages different absences lacuna drawn
in the face of the world or she is singing
as a crane there is no one there every forest
placidly sentient bereft of sentience

many times you have seen your body
as light as many a desiccated patch
of turf torn from a meadow

cells abandon their prescription
clouds enter the body

the only sound is march lilies
decomposing a million years before

SEMAPHORE TO MIGRATING CRANES CIRCLING UNDECIDED
ABOVE THE CONFLUENCE OF TWO RIVERS

this departure unending shadows streaming south humans
into earth ash souls balls

spasms away through constellations unreasonable
exhalations of life spent watching in mountains

granite grow or memorizing vernacular
fungi thinking beneath strolling feet

movements of cloud ideas how
what is wild hides

snow to grandsons talking down ellipses in cloud
dirt roads into bright ruins built

in homage to bent sunlight even here where
dog barks magpie flies teeth fall autumn

falls leaves light memory of before that
what-was-before this

she grooms light into hair moon
comb thousand teeth chattering

found you where willows reside perhaps woman
perhaps willowwind articulated before storm's moon

combed foliage green speech windfall's offspring
wandering stricken by bombardment billion

stars apologized to sky wings rotated
as if miming goodnight to blackness and sky

open window odor of golden
leaves arpeggios through darkness

debris of world's wreckage vacancy untying turpentine never
birthing/killing but banal erosion

thousands year old horned snake's stone erodes by ice
wind rifleshots or from being glimpsed too casually often

even sun regrets its own rasping own soprano detritus
in movement of what could be into inertia vague

misgiving by cosmos
by those who believe

~ ~ ~

KINGFISHER AS DRAGONFLY

this was fallen the way any measure of arrest
is fallen toward horizon any horizon of closure with string delineating

sectors of sky where your grotesque gestures make you
conductor of waves of white geese washing south toward red

sun dawn church bell ratchets five miles
away still no gate to no yard only

guest local madman opens enters and closes
gate of air against air while you did not

design it this way the way
white wind came down from the barrens bearing

ice like a bandage on the very voice you walk
out at dawn see nothing

but sand and an undulation of stakes beckoning to return
to nowhere your heart-rhythm hissing you imagine only birds

in the eaves yet at this distance you merely assimilate
percussive instruments the apparent mnemonic redundancy

of meadow evaporating green
while conifers vibrate blinding snow

you neither are red amaranth nor are not you
both believe and do not believe that you are sentient you recognize

yet fail to remember your reflected countenance dismiss
all as misapprehension of light name it retinal fallacy where there

are two identical stalks of wild millet swaying amongst weeds these
are self and unself each bear numerically exact clusters of grain small

articulate birds consume as you observe black hairs
on the woman's white arm she is metaphor she speaks gestures

of resignation to a bat circling the ceiling fan she seeks
to create quadrants to evoke space with planes gestured

contours these replications are invocations you believe
the real obscured by a pyre miles in reach yet in recognition of red

black gray you realize these are synonyms so excellent animal you
bow to mountains feeling rents appear in the fabric of your organs

house without space for wandering cloud you observe
horizon cusp of scrub oak fire burst aspen memory

you reach toward that horizon separating
sky bird-flight angle of gold autumn light you clasp

any horizon to love to possess
your hand become horizon as fire burst aspen you hear

cicada whine wind in fern bone breaking sound
is word bearing any ascription all meaning meaning

nothing what the magpie says is obvious hissing man is not
obscure nor ice-snow staccato on pane you cannot speak

sing or think the sounds you hear thinking resemble a mole's
burrowing if you rotate your head slowly the prevailing

breeze will lift your beard or feathers sufficiently
to know your scent's destination as two

ravens' voices rise on thermals fall away into black
specks into canyon speckled by black trees

the trees of the orchard are people strangers
they cannot stoop to reach the water a seasonal

transformation where there is no vacuity on which to paint
singing birds or where rain is a gray animal smothering

aphasia's song head-beating against basalt
or metaphysics yet you feel the leaves outside shaking your hands

are black with the aroma of pitch and above cranes'
white tipped into day's crescent moon believe

spring voices vanish into white-falling black cloud dead
sparrows fallen fruit on orchard floor frozen

black toe tips cheeks white coins stagger to feed
stove glow and lack of light makes blind vulnerable

to light even wielding beam not seeing body
of shadow no language or bird voice no sap rising no

pollen or any speaking house built of weeds cactus bird's
nests who would desire wind falls straight down bestial

still in night there are the sky-forced calls of cranes
or perhaps merely calls of stars

any cloud is always god the way vocabularies mutate into syllogisms
of chant into pastels or goldleaf on closed eyelids not sleep

but a prodigious waking dream where rain is semen earth a ruthless
queen ant resplendent in narcosis mentally singing to lightning

as it dances across the globe you have been declaiming that the map's
winds have blown away your face that the antipodes have sucked

the bile from your gall that dolphins are mocking you miming your
mental incontinence thus you see the god of storm blinded by ice

storm debauched by adoration or the drowned stupefied
by myth-painted lips of the lightning bruised exalted by animal

whimpers of those huddled deaf under oil barrels hoping the staccato
drumming signals their coming to a kingdom of heaven

I walk out at dawn and with each step frozen silver-black earth
cracks black-silver sky

no one either here or there the nude
woman under yellow light of the street

lamp is an idea like her eyes which are shards
of water she cannot speak there is no one

to listen merely the tread of humans observing
being in being movement like an owl which strikes

the window pane at midnight or an errant
drunk attempting to strike clarity into the eyes

of his reflection where I march as perfectly
as her idea to the sound of brass

instruments announcing a sky which is
blond a wind which suffocates an earth which tilts persons

which mouth sounds toward an eclipsed sun
which is merely an exact description of my body

"bone" means to-feed-the-cooking-fire
"cedar" is an incense fuel or coffin

or to decompose in a cedar coffin presumes reincarnation
as rain though "tree" means leaves-scattering-light

the turtle shell fracturing in fire is recitation-of-inevitability
in the same way your burnt scapula describes future eclipses

open-gateway (in the setting of a peach orchard)
is a synonym for mouth

listening the hearer focuses on the speaker's
eyes sight being confirmation-of-sincerity

still a broken magpie wing can
not be a metaphor for cut violin strings just as an ululating

voice cannot be arpeggio-of-cello so you posit dualisms
dry-being/wet-being a kind of genetic drift

thus no-thing can matter as nothing
matters coyote-stripped bones or eulogy-as-spring's

violent winds bushel apricot leaves to dust what is married
to evil is merely gestures of merriment easy thought

seeping like cold through walls a statement
of intent eyes focus on summer's fruit no the mouth-

of-the river is an exit the way your fingers framing
your face is not-window wherein

collective memory blinds the forest around a grey woman
rotating in wind merely a kingfisher feather pirouetting from sky

~ ~ ~

SAUNTER

your mountains were waves rising cobalt
on night blue on black

night ridiculed by directional stars which changed
position behind your seeing

and once you had crossed the first
ascent prayer in hand you forgot

your path of incursion and your face
rejoice back home apples still fall neighbors

bicker even the light from your past
fallen stars still falls even your bramble

gate gestures and conversant gulls
still hop on your depleting

wood pile with laughter you thought
minds arc mercly percussive instruments yet.

no path

no north star

no river-to-light

no beckoning song

only orange pools quivering beneath alien trees

Selected Singing Horse Press Titles

Charles Alexander, *Near Or Random Acts.* 2004, $15.00
Charles Alexander, *At the Edge of the Sea*, 2018, $19
David Antin, *John Cage Uncaged Is Still Cagey.* 2005, $15.00
Rae Armantrout, *Collected Prose.* 2007, $17.00
Rachel Tzvia Back, *A Messenger Comes*, 2012, $15.00
Norman Fischer, *The Strugglers*, 2013, $15.00
Norman Fischer, *Magnolias All At Once*, 2015, $15
Phillip Foss, *The Ideation.* 2004, $15.00
Phillip Foss, *Imperfect Poverty.* 2006, $15.00
Phillip Foss, *The Valley of Cranes.* 2010, $15.00
Mary Rising Higgins, *)cliff TIDES((.* 2005, $15.00
Mary Rising Higgins, *)joule TIDES((.* 2007, $15.00
Lindsay Hill, *Contango.* 2006, $14.00
Lindsay Hill, *The Empty Quarter.* 2010, $15.00
Karen Kelley, *Mysterious Peripheries.* 2006, $15.00
Hank Lazer, *The New Spirit.* 2005, $14.00
Hank Lazer, *N18 (Complete).* 2012, $15
Andrew Mossin, *The Veil.* 2008, $15.00
Paul Naylor, *Playing Well With Others.* 2004, $15.00
Rochelle Owens, *Hermaphropoetics*, 2017, $15
Ed Roberson, *The New Wing of the Labyrinth.* 2009, $15
Ted Pearson, *Extant Glyphs: 1964-1980, 2014. $15*
Ted Pearson, *After Hours, 2016, $15*
Andrew Schelling, *A Possible Bag*, 2013, $15.95
Andrew Schelling, *The Real People of Wind and Rain*, 2014, 18.95
Susan M. Schultz, *Dementia Blog.* 2008, $15.00
Susan M. Schultz, *Memory Cards.* 2011, $15.00
Susan M. Schultz, *"She's Welcome to Her Disease*, 2013, $15.00

These titles are available online at **www.singinghorsepress.com**, or through Small Press Distribution, at (800) 869-7553 or online at **www.spdbooks.org**